STORY HOUR

GREEN SAYS GO

BY ED EMBERLEY

Boston   LITTLE, BROWN AND COMPANY   Toronto

Let me tell you some things about colors and their
names. There are three primary colors: Red, yellow,
and blue.

LIBRARY OF CONGRESS CATALOG CARD NO. 68 – 21165

Seventh Printing

Published simultaneously in Canada by Little, Brown & Company (Canada) Limited

With these three colors plus black and white you can
make any color you like. This book is printed in red,
yellow, blue, and black on white paper.

There are three secondary colors:
Orange, green, and purple.

The three secondary colors are made by mixing the three primary colors. Red and yellow make orange, yellow and blue make green, and red and blue make purple. You cannot make red, yellow, or blue by mixing any other colors. . . . Try it.

To make colors lighter, mix white with them. When you mix white with blue, green, orange, yellow, or purple, you call them light blue, light green, light orange, light yellow, and light purple.

Two light colors have special names. Light red is called pink, and light black is called gray. I don't think I have ever heard anyone say "light red," and I know I have never heard anyone say "light black." Have you?

To make colors darker, mix black with them. When you mix black with blue, green, yellow, red, or purple, you call them dark blue, dark green, dark yellow, dark red, and dark purple.

Two dark colors have special names. Dark white is called gray, and dark orange is called brown. Are you surprised that brown is just dark orange?

Now that you know some of their names let's look at some of the things that colors say.

On a traffic light, green says "GO."

Yellow says "Watch out
I'm going to change to red" and red says "STOP."

12   On a car, white says "I am coming toward you."

Red says "I am going away from you."

Here blue says "I am a police car."

And here red says "I am a fire engine or ambulance."

On a boat, red says "port" and green says "starboard."

Purple says "I'm angry."

White says "I'm afraid."

Red says "I'm embarrassed."

Green says "I'm jealous."

Blue says "I'm sad."

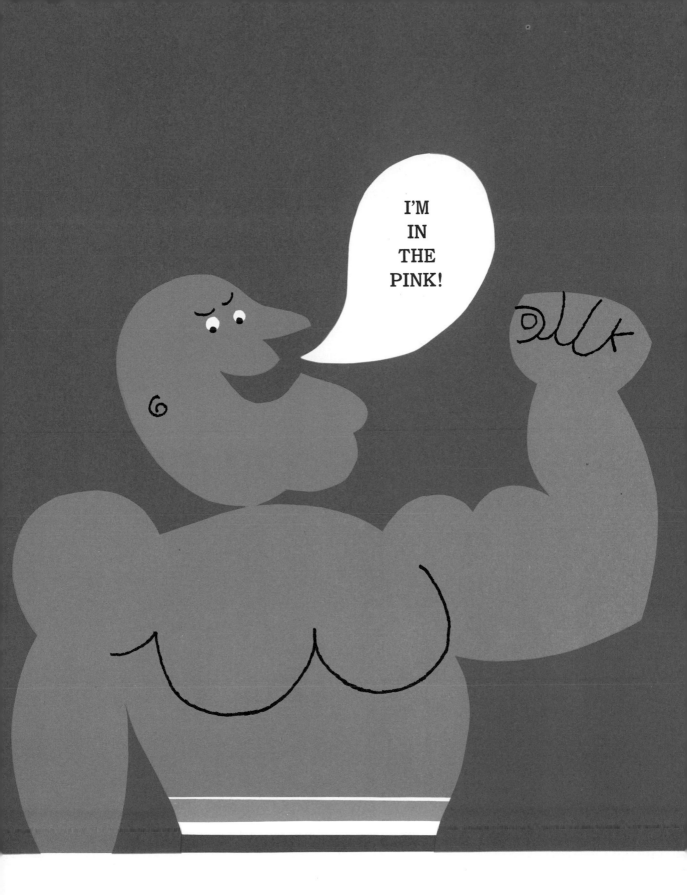

Pink says "I feel great."

On a baby, pink says "I'm a girl."

Blue says "I'm a boy."

Black and orange say "It's Halloween."

Red and green say "It's Christmas."

These are not all the things that colors say. I have left some for you to find or make up. For instance: What colors say Easter? Thanksgiving? Fourth of July? Valentine's Day? What color says hot? cold? sick? summer? fall? winter? spring? Can you think of a fruit that has the same name as a color? Can you think of a flower that has the same name as a color? People feel blue, green, or yellow, but do they ever feel orange? gray? brown? or white?

Think about it sometime.

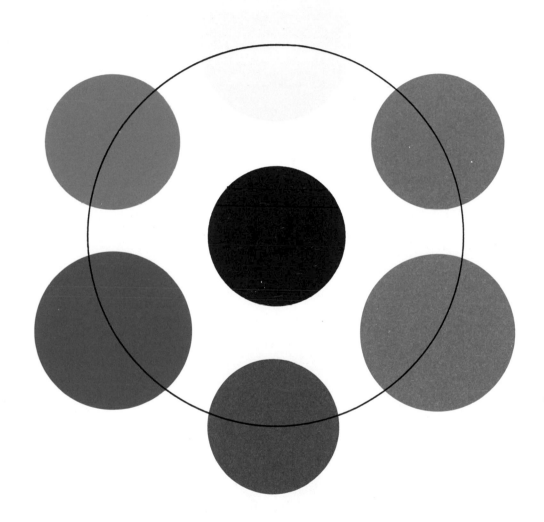